Meditations for
Deeper Trust

JUST A MINUTE

Meditations for
Deeper Trust

By Kathryn J. Hermes, FSP

Pauline
BOOKS & MEDIA
Boston

Library of Congress Cataloging-in-Publication Data

Names: Hermes, Kathryn, author.

Title: Meditations for deeper trust / by Kathryn J. Hermes, FSP.

Description: Boston : Pauline Books & Media, [2018] | "This book has been excerpted from Cherished by the Lord (Pauline Books & Media, 2012)."

Identifiers: LCCN 2018021772| ISBN 9780819849786 (pbk.) | ISBN 0819849782 (pbk.)

Subjects: LCSH: Trust in God--Christianity--Meditations. | LCGFT: Devotional literature.

Classification: LCC BV4637 .H47 2018 | DDC 242/.2--dc23

LC record available at https://lccn.loc.gov/2018021772

This book has been excerpted from *Cherished by the Lord* (Pauline Books & Media, 2012).

Cover design by Rosana Usselmann

Published by Pauline Books & Media, 50 Saint Pauls Avenue, Boston, MA 02130-3491. www.pauline.org

Printed in the U.S.A.

Pauline Books & Media is the publishing house of the Daughters of St. Paul, an international congregation of women religious serving the Church with the communications media.

2 3 4 5 6 7 8 9   23 22 21 20 19

Introduction

When someone encourages you to trust in God, do you feel like you've tried to, but you just can't seem to do it?

Trust is not something we do or achieve through our effort; it's a *response* to what God has done and is doing. In this book we will meditate on the *evidence* of God's trustworthiness, as shown in the Bible. Once we see proof of God's caring action in salvation history, we can also see it in our own history. Our trust then flows from being convinced that God is steadfast and reliable.

The meditations in this book are my go-to scripture meditation and prayers when I'm overwhelmed with life and the devil tries to make me believe I'm on my own. When I read them, I know with a deep-down surety that I'm valuable in God's eyes and that he is glad he created me . . . and there is no way he will let me fall from his hands. Scripture is the way we connect to God's heart, where we are astounded as God tells us what he thinks about us. And it is amazing!

So here is an easy method of reading these meditations that I use. It will unlock in your heart the courage to believe in God's desire to save and bless you in all things:

1. God will lead you to be interested in certain meditations. Go wherever God leads you. You don't have to read these in order unless you'd like to.

2. Before you read, stop and remember a moment when someone delighted in having you around. Tell God how grateful you are for that gift of love.

3. Begin to read the meditation. Relish what you read. Notice the words and phrases that seem to light a fire that warms your heart. Enjoy the safety and beauty of that moment.

4. Talk to God about what is burdening you right now. Then reread the words of Scripture in the meditation, hearing them as if God were speaking them to you by name. Even place your name right in the passage and imagine God speaking these words to you directly. Notice what it is like and tell God how grateful you are.

My wish for you is that you place yourself before the Lord as an empty canvas, trusting that in all things the divine Artist of your life will paint the story of his love for you in both bright and dark colors, with both delicate and bold strokes.

How Great Is God's Love

See what love the Father has bestowed on us that we may be called the children of God. Yet so we are. The reason the world does not know us is that it did not know him. Beloved, we are God's children now; what we shall be has not yet been revealed. We do know that when it is revealed we shall be like him, for we shall see him as he is. Everyone who has this hope based on him makes himself pure, as he is pure.

1 Jn 3:1–3 (NABRE)

———— • ◦ • • ————

Jesus' last will and testament was that his disciples would see and *share* in the glory that he has with the Father. Thus, this seeing becomes *participation*. We watch movies about Jesus or read the Scriptures. We may often feel like we are "on the outside looking in." In reality, though, God has loved us with an extravagant, undeserved love. We have been granted a share in God's life through the Holy Spirit who has been poured into our hearts. The

Spirit within us is the guarantee that our participation in the life of God will not end in disgrace. God himself has given us the promise and is quickening within us the divine life to come. God himself will keep his promise in us. This is a consolation for all those who mourn and worry about their loved ones who have left the practice of their faith or who no longer believe in God. Ask God to fulfill his promises to us, to give us the first fruits of salvation already sown in our lives at our Baptism through the Spirit's gift. We are called to abide in the Spirit's love within us, and God will chase after the person who runs from his love.

In your hands, my God, I place all those who flee from you. Let their journey ultimately end up in your arms.

The Riddle of Our Existence

Blessed be the Lord God of Israel,
>   for he has looked favorably on his people
>   and redeemed them.
He has raised up a mighty savior for us
>   in the house of his servant David,
as he spoke through the mouth of his holy
>   prophets from of old,
>   that we would be saved from our enemies
>   and from the hand of all who hate us.
Thus he has shown the mercy promised to our
>   ancestors,
>   and has remembered his holy covenant,
the oath that he swore to our ancestor
>   Abraham. . . .

LK 1:68–73

This Gospel passage reveals a lot about God's
work and his creative love. Luke uses words of
mercy and words of *action*. Sometimes we wonder
where God is. Those who bear great sorrow in their

hearts can often find themselves overwhelmed by questions and loneliness. Where is God? What does it all mean? Zechariah's canticle, however, proclaims that God *is* mercy and action. God never promised to rescue his people from the human condition. Instead he did something so wondrous we could never comprehend it: the Father sent the Son to *share* our human condition *with us*. He was born. He grew up. He suffered. He was betrayed. He was alone. He died. And he rose from death and ascended into heaven *where we are now able to follow.*

Jesus, you showed us that what we experience as the human condition does not contain the key to the riddle of our existence. Only Love does. Help us to gradually become strong enough to love even in the midst of disappointment and pain. May we share in the power of your salvific love, that we might discover the ultimate meaning of our lives.

How God Slips into Life

Again he entered the synagogue, and a man was
there who had a withered hand. They watched
him to see whether he would cure him on the
sabbath, so that they might accuse him. And he
said to the man who had the withered hand,
"Come forward." Then he said to them, "Is it
lawful to do good or to do harm on the sabbath,
to save life or to kill?" But they were silent. He
looked around at them with anger; he was
grieved at their hardness of heart and said to the
man, "Stretch out your hand." He stretched it
out, and his hand was restored. The Pharisees
went out and immediately conspired with the
Herodians against him, how to destroy him.

MK 3:1–6

Reading this Gospel passage, it is easy to forget
that it was as a member of the Jewish community that Jesus claimed to have the authority to
do what God alone can do—forgive sins. Jesus'

activity and teaching must have baffled his contemporaries. They struggled to figure out exactly who he was and why he thought he had the authority to do what he did. Those who watched him carefully in the synagogue that day hoped to gather enough evidence to accuse him. They had lost the open wonder and amazement at God's power, which they had witnessed when Jesus healed the paralytic. Now they were no longer inquirers, observers, or disciples, but his judges. They had made up their minds that the words of this rabbi couldn't possibly be from God. It is so easy for me to slip from being disciple to judge. Every time I put myself, my comfort, my ideas, or my excuses before obedience I am no longer a disciple. Instead, I have put myself in the place of judging the worth of Jesus' teaching and examples. I forget that God slips into my life in baffling ways, turning my values and judgments on their head.

Lord, help me to remain amazed and not angered by you who interfere with my pride and my plans, trusting that you know what you desire to make of me and how you plan to use me. Amen.

The God Who Promises

For everything there is a season, and a time for
  every matter under heaven:
    a time to be born, and a time to die;
    a time to plant, and a time to pluck up
    what is planted;
    a time to kill, and a time to heal;
    a time to break down, and a time to build
        up;
    a time to weep, and a time to laugh;
    a time to mourn, and a time to dance . . .
    a time to seek, and a time to lose . . .
    a time to keep silence, and a time to speak;
    a time to love, and a time to hate;
    a time for war, and a time for peace.

ECCL 3:1–4, 6–8

———— ◦ • • • ◦ ————

These verses from Ecclesiastes form one of the
Bible's best-loved passages. There is a time for
everything under the sun. God has created an
orderly world in which he has made everything

suitable for its time. Yet the author of Ecclesiastes complains later on in the chapter that from the beginning to the end we cannot discover what God has done. God hasn't let us in on his secrets. Throughout salvation history God has called people to play a part in the story of his love: Noah, Abraham, Moses, Isaiah, John the Baptist, Mary, the Apostle Paul. Each of these people would attest that God had something in mind when he called them. But God didn't give them all the details of how it would be worked out. God does not work with strategic plans. He makes promises and leads his chosen people on winding paths that often seem to make little sense. God has also made promises to us. Faith in God's promises—and in the *God who promises*—makes the difference between seeing the situations of our life as random, hostile events or the mysterious expression of Divine Providence.

I place myself before you, Lord, as an empty canvas—paint on it the story of your love for me in both bright and dark colors, with both delicate and bold strokes. Be the artist of my life.

I Forbid You to Fear

Immediately he made the disciples get into the boat and go on ahead to the other side, while he dismissed the crowds. And after he had dismissed the crowds, he went up the mountain by himself to pray. When evening came, he was there alone, but by this time the boat, battered by the waves, was far from the land, for the wind was against them. And early in the morning he came walking toward them on the sea. But when the disciples saw him walking on the sea, they were terrified, saying, "It is a ghost!" And they cried out in fear. But immediately Jesus spoke to them and said, "Take heart, it is I; do not be afraid."

Mt 14:22–27

＊ ＊ ＊ ＊

A friend of mine speaks, somewhat resentfully, about her pains: "Jesus suffered, so that means I have to suffer too." The disciples' cry of fear from the midst of a situation that threatens destruction would be just another one of those proofs that we can't expect anything better of life than suffering. Somehow, however, this type of reasoning makes God at once the cause of evil and the One who has no power or desire to save us. What we see in this Gospel passage, instead, is the divine way in which God turns the tables on his disciples to teach us to see things from the divine perspective. From the center of a situation of fear and danger—a situation that he has allowed in their lives—Jesus does two things. First Jesus states, *I forbid you to go on fearing from this point forward*, and second, he *approaches* the boat. Jesus walks straight toward us in our personal crisis into the *midst* of the fearful situation. God shows us that his love is more powerful than the dangers around us, and in our sufferings we can discover him taking up his abode in our frightened hearts and commanding, "Do not be afraid!"

Come, Jesus, right into the midst of my struggles. In every crisis may I see you and fear no more.

The Vision Has Its Time

Are you not from of old, O LORD,
    my holy God, immortal?
LORD, you have appointed them for judgment,
    O Rock, you have set them in place to
        punish!
Your eyes are too pure to look upon wickedness,
    and the sight of evil you cannot endure.
Why, then, do you gaze on the faithless in silence
    while the wicked devour those more just
        than themselves?

HAB 1:12–13 (NABRE)

At any one point how many millions of people are probably saying these very words to God? People who have been swindled of their money, seen loved ones lose life or limb because of another's careless or criminal activity, had to forfeit career or reputation, or been left with psychological wounds too terrible to bear from another's sinful behavior. Why, O God, do you sit by and do nothing to protect your loved ones? The next lines of this passage are perhaps the only answer: "For the vision is a witness for the appointed time . . . if it delays, wait for it, it will surely come . . . the just one who is righteous because of faith shall live" (Hab 2:2–4). Jesus himself, hanging on the Cross, had to wait for God's vindication. He surrendered his life in complete trust of his Father. Jesus trusted even though it seemed like he was left alone in the most pitiable circumstances. Three days he lay in the darkness of the tomb. Then God raised him up in glory. Jesus proved to us that God can be trusted. We can be sure, no matter what has gone wrong in our lives, that "the just one who is righteous because of faith shall live" (Hab 2:4).

My heart breaks when I see another suffer and often I have no words to say. Sometimes my own faith in you, my God, is shaken. Strengthen my belief in you!

The Lord Comes in Strength

"Everyone then who hears these words of mine and acts on them will be like a wise man who built his house on rock. The rain fell, the floods came, and the winds blew and beat on that house, but it did not fall, because it had been founded on rock. And everyone who hears these words of mine and does not act on them will be like a foolish man who built his house on sand. The rain fell, and the floods came, and the winds blew and beat against that house, and it fell— and great was its fall!"

MT 7:24–27

———— ❖ • • ❖ ————

Raise your voice and tell the Good News: the Lord our God comes in strength! This Gospel passage about the rainy season gives us an image of strength, with the torrents and winds that tested the houses of both the wise and foolish. I hear accounts of these torrents and winds in people's lives over and over again, every single day: financial difficulties, unexpected illnesses, relationship failures, employment problems. Indeed, the Gospel's rainy season comes to each of our lives at one time or another. Whether we are in that season right now or not, we need to test the foundation of our lives. Is it strong? Has the "house" of our life been built on the solid rock of faith and obedient love? The torrents and winds come crashing into life in this fallen world, but the Good News is that as strong as they may blow, and as hard as they may buffet our hearts, the Lord our God is stronger! Truly, "we have a strong city" (Isa 26:1).

Lord, it is true. My life has seen strong winds and torrential downpours that I feared would destroy me. But you were stronger. I praise you forever.

Transforming Disaster
into Life

After saying this Jesus was troubled in spirit, and
declared, "Very truly, I tell you, one of you will
betray me." . . . "Lord, who is it?" Jesus answered,
"It is the one to whom I give this piece of bread
when I have dipped it in the dish." So when he
had dipped the piece of bread, he gave it to Judas
son of Simon Iscariot. After he received the piece
of bread, Satan entered into him. Jesus said to
him, "Do quickly what you are going to do."

JN 13:21, 25–27

It is instinctive for humans to seek to preserve
their life. We marvel at and give honors to persons who put their life in jeopardy to save another.
In this Gospel passage, Jesus steps out of the very
human pattern of self-preservation, yet we almost
miss it. Jesus sees the dark clouds gathering on the
horizon. Still, Jesus gives Judas permission to leave

the table and go into the night to accomplish the plans he harbors in his heart. Jesus lets him go. No persuasion to change his mind. No last-minute attempts to win Judas over. No underhanded statements to alert the other Apostles to the impending catastrophe. Jesus simply tells Judas to go and accomplish his plans quickly. What must Jesus have felt as his eyes followed this hand-picked Apostle with whom he had shared so many blessed experiences over the past three years? Jesus watched sadly as the man rose from the table, looked furtively around, and backed out of the room, closing the door firmly behind him. At times we are in a similar predicament. A painful situation enters our life and with dignity we live it fully, trusting in the Father's overarching goodness, which alone can transform disaster into life.

Today I take a moment to connect the dots in my life—yes, Lord, you have been good. The painful moments and days have left me with a treasure. The darkness has led me to light and life. Thank you.

Allow Mary to Hold You

Guided by the Spirit, Simeon came into the temple; and when the parents brought in the child Jesus, to do for him what was customary under the law, Simeon took him in his arms and praised God. . . . And the child's father and mother were amazed at what was being said about him. Then Simeon blessed them and said to his mother Mary, "This child is destined for the falling and the rising of many in Israel, and to be a sign that will be opposed so that the inner thoughts of many will be revealed—and a sword will pierce your own soul too."

LK 2:27–28, 33–35

Our grown children suffer from depression, eating disorders, divorce, loneliness, financial disaster. . . . The list could go on and on. But for a mother's heart it is more than a list. It is the prospect of her child's life swirling out of control, of the family's attention and resources being swallowed up by the incalculable and unforgiveable. In the temple where she presented her Son to the Lord, Mary's heart was also shaken by the vision of what form that "sword" could take. She walked with her child through the joys and pains of his life, and stood before the "failure" and utter disappointment of the crucifixion. Mary, like every sorrowful mother, somehow had the faith to believe in her Son even as she held his dead body and laid it in a grave. To believe, yes, and with oh so much love, to hold the image of his face in her heart. She, above all women, knows a mother's sorrows. If you are sorrowing or you know a mother who is, pick up a life of the Blessed Mother, your rosary, the Scriptures, and allow her to hold you, as only a mother can, in your sorrow.

I take you, Mary, to be my mother. Walk with me in the joys and sorrows of my life. Amen.

God Alone Saves

Blessed be the LORD, my rock,
>   who trains my hands for war, and my
>   fingers for battle;
my rock and my fortress,
>   my stronghold and my deliverer,
my shield, in whom I take refuge,
>   who subdues the peoples under me.
O LORD, what are human beings that you
    regard them,
>   or mortals that you think of them?
They are like a breath;
>   their days are like a passing shadow.

Ps 144:1–4

——— • • • • ———

Tragedy is never far from the human condition. We experience it personally and live through tragic times as a family, community, or nation. Fear, illness, depression, abuse, and financial disaster are at our heels. We fend them off, look for lucky breaks, try whatever will keep us beyond their reach. Sometimes prayer can be reduced to asking for help for ourselves, our families, friends, and neighbors. This psalm offers us a way to pray in those tragic times. It begins with the king stating his dependence on God. God is a safeguard, our fortress, our stronghold, our deliverer. We can trust God. God is the one who gives kings their victory. God will rescue. These words were no doubt written at a time of crisis that threatened the future of the king and the people. I have seen people go through tremendous times of pain and crisis. The only thing that we can know to be true at those moments is that God *is* faithful. That God alone saves. That God walks with us through our dark valleys and hangs with us on our crosses. We wait for God to appear, only to discover that he is already with us and we are not alone. In our deepest pain we can trust that he is working to save.

O faithful Love, walk with me through both sorrow and joy. Let me see your face and I shall be saved.

Keep Watch

I will stand at my watchpost,
>and station myself on the rampart;
I will keep watch to see what he will say to me,
>and what he will answer concerning my
>>complaint.
Then the LORD answered me and said:
Write the vision;
>make it plain on tablets. . . .
For there is still a vision for the appointed time;
>it speaks of the end, and does not lie.
If it seems to tarry, wait for it;
>it will surely come, it will not delay.
Look at the proud!
>Their spirit is not right in them,
>but the righteous live by their faith.

HAB 2:1–4

———— ◆ · ◆ · ◆ ————

When Habakkuk became a prophet, the Israelites were struggling with a desperate situation. In this passage, Habakkuk complains to God, and then says, *All right, I am going to see how the Lord responds. I am going to sit here until I get an answer.* The prophet dares to address God with boldness and assurance.

While reflecting on Habakkuk's prayer, I received a phone call from a woman who often asks for prayers. She told me she had only ten dollars left in her wallet. An abusive husband had left her with no home and no sense of self-worth. She had no job. She was afraid. Desperate. Lonely. She was in a place of insecurity, the depth of which I will probably never experience. After talking and praying together, we could say only one thing. *We shall station ourselves at our post and see what God does.* It's easy to trust God when a financial cushion separates us from living on the streets. In this desperate situation, however, can God *really* come through? Does God *really* care about us? These questions tear at the souls of Christians today. As the rich become richer and the poor become more desperate, where is God for them, for us? How will God save? *Let us see what the Lord will do. Let us wait here until we get an answer.*

Lord of the vision, promise of the future, come, do not tarry.

We Depend on Miracles

Then suddenly a woman who had been suffering from hemorrhages for twelve years came up behind him and touched the fringe of his cloak, for she said to herself, "If I only touch his cloak, I will be made well." Jesus turned, and seeing her he said, "Take heart, daughter; your faith has made you well." And instantly the woman was made well.

Mt 9:20–22

———•·••·•———

This unnamed woman who approaches Jesus with her need symbolizes each of us. We too totally depend on miracles. We can't heal ourselves. We can't fix our problems. Just like this woman, we seek help from doctors and experts in so many areas—medicine, psychology, science, physics, strategic planning, government, law, education, time management. . . . Each has its place. Each contributes something wonderful to the development of this world. But in the end, we must approach God as the ultimate power of love, who alone can sustain our existence. Our existence rests on the hands of grace. Of ourselves we can only *receive* life and give thanks for it as a continuous gift. Our most authentic posture as a part of God's creation is that of this woman suffering from hemorrhages: "If only I can touch him, I shall be saved." It is her faith, her courage, her determination, her risk to show her need, her desire for health, and her realization of God's infinite superiority over the world that we must claim for our own if we are to receive, like her, true healing and life.

Infinite Love of our God! If only I could know you, if only I could touch you, I would be healed!

Two Things We Can Trust

Now the whole earth had one language and the
same words. And . . . they came upon a plain in
the land of Shinar and settled there. Then they
said, "Come, let us build ourselves a city, and a
tower with its top in the heavens, and let us make
a name for ourselves. . . ." The LORD came down
to see the city and the tower, which mortals had
built. And the LORD said, "Look, they are one
people, and they have all one language . . . nothing that they propose to do will now be
impossible for them. Come, let us go down, and
confuse their language there, so that they will
not understand one another's speech." So the
LORD scattered them abroad . . . and they left off
building the city.

GEN 11:1–2, 4–8

--- • • • • ---

T he people building the city of Babel were a bit
pretentious. They were planning to build their
lives and their city on their own, for their own ends.
If we are honest, however, probably all of us have

fallen into this very human tendency. Often when we are forced to stop because of sickness, failure, or obstacles, we begin to resonate with deeper values and our life has more meaning. God leaves us with something beautiful even as he prevents us from building our own lives and cities without him.

But this is not the end of the story. In the Acts of the Apostles, after the Spirit descended upon Mary and the Apostles, Peter spoke to those gathered in Jerusalem. Although these people spoke different languages, they could all understand Peter's message (see Acts 2). Now *God* was building the city, and continuing to live in our midst through the Spirit. At times we cannot understand why God has let something happen. We can always trust two things, however: first, we can always learn something from it, no matter how unfair the situation; and second, if we allow God to "build the city," we do not have to be afraid because God will work things out for our good.

Lord, direct my life. Free me from the pride that would lead me to build up my life for my own glory. Help me instead to live for you. Amen.

To Love Is to Risk

For God is love.

1 Jn 4:8

⬦ • ⬦ • ⬦

Love is the life of God. We came forth from loving hands. After we had broken God's trust in the garden, God mercifully clothed us (see Gen 3:21). Love has madly pursued us, collectively and individually. Love died as nothing on the Cross, transferring to us the gift of the Father's love. We have been bought at a price by Love for love. If we truly live, we live of love. If we are truly human, we are love. Love, human and divine, is fragile. Its only power is the power of forgiveness, the power of those who wait, who search, who desire. It is not the power of military might, commerce, or lust. Love plays a different song. Trusting love's music is hard. The song of Love can be threatened by the cacophony of fear, insecurity, and need. The enticements of power and security will crack the wall of love's edifice and erode its foundation of love.. To love is to risk. Not to love is to risk even more. It is a choice, a choice to forgive, to give to a selfish person, to be with an older person who needs a friend, to work on a relationship with a friend or spouse. Loving is the life of God . . . loving is authentic living.

Jesus, lover of all humanity, Love of my soul, break the shell of my boredom that I might be love in the world.

Have Absolute Confidence

And when he got into the boat, his disciples followed him. A windstorm arose on the sea, so
great that the boat was being swamped by the
waves; but he was asleep. And they went and
woke him up, saying, "Lord, save us! We are per-
ishing!" And he said to them, "Why are you
afraid, you of little faith?" Then he got up and
rebuked the winds and the sea; and there was a
dead calm. They were amazed, saying, "What
sort of man is this, that even the winds and the
sea obey him?"

Mt 8:23–27

———•·•·•———

When I was in my thirties and finishing my
theology degree, I remember being con-
cerned that ill health might cut my life short—that
all my education might never be used. Perhaps it
was a subtle anxiety that I might never make my
mark on the world. Recently I've caught myself
confiding to God that I wouldn't mind if he took

me today or tomorrow. Life doesn't allow one to build a monument to the Lord, much less to one-self. More and more I find myself simply worshiping, surrendering in the moment, not needing to grasp it, build on it, categorize it. The moment can pass, just like every other present moment, because all that is necessary will be given to me. Someone once told me she wanted to be able to sleep as Jesus had in the boat during the storms of life. At the time it struck me as a creative under-standing of that Gospel passage. Now I think I'm finally beginning to understand what she meant—absolute confidence, in the face of life or death, to remain at peace.

In life and in death I am yours, O Lord. I need nothing else but to love you forever.

So Be It

Truly, O people in Zion, inhabitants of Jerusalem, you shall weep no more. He will surely be gracious to you at the sound of your cry; when he hears it, he will answer you. . . .

He will give rain for the seed with which you sow the ground, and grain, the produce of the ground, which will be rich and plenteous. . . . [T]he light of the moon will be like the light of the sun, and the light of the sun will be sevenfold, like the light of seven days, on the day when the LORD binds up the injuries of his people, and heals the wounds inflicted by his blow.

ISA 30:19, 23, 26

———— ·•·• ————

For some people I know, it seems like God never speaks to them and their souls are filled with a stuffy darkness. The stars have gone out. They can't hear even a hint of the melody of God's language. They suffer because they feel God doesn't care to save them from this uncomfortable, exhausting agony. Throughout Scripture we see individuals in this situation, peering into the darkness for a sign of God's care for them. This passage expresses that human yearning. The coming of Jesus is the fullest answer to our longing to see the light through the darkness, whatever our darkness may be. After Jesus' coming we can never doubt that God is with us, bending over us with care, even though we know him not.

O Silent One, Light in my darkness, Light I cannot see, Fire whose warmth I cannot feel, if I may not feel your presence, so be it. I'll remain unblinking in your dark presence. I will stand at the ready as the mystic silence of your love penetrates my heart. I know that dawn will come. Dawn must break. But until the first streaks of light pierce the night and turn it into morning, I will live in faith that you are here, beside me. You know. You care. Whatever way you wish to be with me, so be it. I will remain with you. Amen.

Father

He was praying in a certain place, and after he had finished, one of his disciples said to him, "Lord, teach us to pray, as John taught his disciples." He said to them, "When you pray, say: Father, hallowed be your name. Your kingdom come. Give us each day our daily bread. And forgive us our sins, for we ourselves forgive everyone indebted to us. And do not bring us to the time of trial."

Lk 11:1–4

———•·••·•———

The first word of the prayer we all learned as children, the Lord's Prayer, reminds me of the first article of the Creed: I believe in God, the *Father*. It seems to me that the "practical" parts of the Our Father—give us our daily bread, forgive us our sins, do not put us to the test—get more attention than this one most important word that stands at its head: *Father*. Jesus didn't say, *God, may your name be held holy*. He said, "Father." This word indicates a relationship—a relationship of birth and of love, of life and of connection. It tells us simultaneously who God is and who we are. It signifies that God is not a force, not an idea, and not a far away regent who rules by law and punishment. God has a face, just as every father has a face. When we say "Father," we declare ourselves to be children. We exist in a filial relationship with God—safe, secure, wanted, loved, and gazed upon. We declare that we are dependent, that we too are called to love. And out of this love we desire to obey. Obedience is but a sign of our love.

May your kingdom come!

Breaking Bread

Now on that same day two of them were going to a village called Emmaus. . . . As they came near the village to which they were going, he walked ahead as if he were going on. But they urged him strongly, saying, "Stay with us, because it is almost evening and the day is now nearly over." So he went in to stay with them. When he was at the table with them, he took bread, blessed and broke it, and gave it to them. Then their eyes were opened, and they recognized him; and he vanished from their sight. They said to each other, "Were not our hearts burning within us while he was talking to us on the road . . . ?"

Lᴋ 24:13, 28–32

◆—◆·◆·◆—◆

Good Friday and Holy Saturday have always been days when I soberly remember the passion and death of the Lord, but I have not often lived the vulnerability Jesus must have experienced. The tragic terrorist attacks in New York and

Washington, DC, on September 11, 2001, were an experience of this vulnerability. Any illusion of control I thought I possessed over my life, the future, or the safety of those I love was ripped away from me. That Easter was the first Easter I celebrated in the state of mind and heart of the disciples walking toward Emmaus, grieving and confused by the rapid succession of events in Jerusalem. Perhaps you have experienced this yourself. Experiences of home foreclosure, fear of losing a job, the inability to restore a loved one to health, financial disaster— all these are moments of Holy Saturday vulnerability. This delightful Gospel passage reveals to us the fidelity of God in the midst of chaotic darkness. Jesus met these two friends of his, listened to them, and broke bread with them. In this action, he healed and renewed them. We may never be able to put our worlds back together as they once were. Like the two Emmaus disciples, we can't go back to the way it was before. But in the breaking of the bread we can go forward.

Jesus, you are alive! You, the fidelity of God, are my hope and my future.

Simple Stories

Now a man from the house of Levi went and
married a Levite woman. The woman conceived
and bore a son; and when she saw that he was a
fine baby, she hid him three months. When she
could hide him no longer she got a papyrus bas-
ket for him, and plastered it with bitumen and
pitch; she put the child in it and placed it among
the reeds on the bank of the river. His sister
stood at a distance, to see what would happen to
him . . . [Pharaoh's daughter] took him as her
son. She named him Moses, "because," she said,
"I drew him out of the water."

Ex 2:1–4, 10

- • · · • -

Under the shadow of Pharaoh's crushing power
and oppression of the Hebrew people, one
small Levite family fell in love with their baby boy
and hid him from the authorities. Such a simple
story, but for those of us who are sometimes overwhelmed by the power of government, the tragedy

of war, and the news of famine and oppression, the story of Moses is a paradigm. God is here. God is present and active in our world. God does mighty things through small, everyday actions. God doesn't need attention, troops, or announcements. God works in little ways, ways so hidden that we barely notice them. In fact, we can hardly believe that the small things of our lives are part of the glorious drama of salvation. I'm sure Moses' mother was glad that she had saved her son's life. She couldn't have known, however, that she had saved the one who would set her people free. Such a simple story—as simple as our own. Often, we too have no idea how the simple things we do will affect others.

Mighty God, Guardian of our lives, use the simple things I do to accomplish the mystery of your plan of love and salvation.

Getting God's Attention

"Ask and it will be given to you; seek and you will find; knock and the door will be opened to you. For everyone who asks, receives; and the one who seeks, finds; and to the one who knocks, the door will be opened. Which one of you would hand his son a stone when he asks for a loaf of bread, or a snake when he asks for a fish? If you then, who are wicked, know how to give good gifts to your children, how much more will your heavenly Father give good things to those who ask him."

MT 7:7–11 (NABRE)

Retreats, holy hours, novenas, prayer chains. . . . All of these in some way hearken back to this promise of Jesus: *Ask, seek, knock, and what you desire will be yours.* Whether we are asking for material or spiritual blessings for others or for ourselves, this image of prayer reminds us of children attempting to get God's attention. Indeed, the parental image of God is suggested by Jesus himself, "Which one of you would hand his son a stone?" One day God said to me, *Everything you need I've already given you.* These seven words flipped my spiritual life on its head! God was saying that the present moment contains everything I need. After we ask, seek, and knock, we need to thank, receive, and enjoy. God *also* calls us to be perfectly happy with what we have received. After all, a good parent will give more to a child who appreciates what he or she has been given.

Father of Jesus and my Father, I thank you for all that has been in my life, for all that is, and for all that will be.

Come, Lord Jesus

John to the seven churches that are in Asia:
Grace to you and peace from him who is and
who was and who is to come, and from the seven
spirits who are before his throne, and from Jesus
Christ, the faithful witness, the firstborn of the
dead, and the ruler of the kings of the earth. To
him who loves us and freed us from our sins by
his blood, and made us to be a kingdom, priests
serving his God and Father, to him be glory and
dominion forever and ever. Amen. . . . "I am the
Alpha and the Omega," says the Lord God, who
is and who was and who is to come, the Almighty.

REV 1:4–6, 8

◆ ◆ ◆ ◆ ◆

The Book of Revelation is a comforting guide to
Christians of every age. John warns that we
must contend with the powers of the world we live
in. We deal with the values of a society often far
from Christian, with all the problems of a complex
and confusing technological era. We *can* do many

things, but is it morally right to do them? We will contend with the principalities of the world until the close of history. Jesus Christ, the faithful witness, sees everything. Let this passage give you a bit of confidence. Let it pierce the darkness you may see around you with a shaft of light falling from the open door of eternity. But remember that the beginning of the Book of Revelation does not castigate the rulers of Babylon and the emperors of Rome. Instead it speaks quite strongly to the Christians in the seven churches in Asia. This corrects our perceptions that the problem is all "out there" in the darkness. The Book of Revelation calls us to be more of who we already are, to give the Lord glory and dominion in our lives, to let him be the Alpha and the Omega of our personal history.

Come, Lord Jesus, come, now, here. Come into my heart. Come into the world. Come transform our history. Come, Lord Jesus, come!

Nothing Is Arbitrary

The LORD said to Abram, after Lot had separated from him, "Raise your eyes now, and look from the place where you are, northward and southward and eastward and westward; for all the land that you see I will give to you and to your offspring forever. I will make your offspring like the dust of the earth; so that if one can count the dust of the earth, your offspring also can be counted. Rise up, walk through the length and the breadth of the land, for I will give it to you." So Abram moved his tent, and came and settled by the oaks of Mamre, which are at Hebron; and there he built an altar to the LORD.

GEN 13:14–18

Sometimes my life can seem arbitrary. "We need a person with a degree in this role, will you accept a transfer?" "We don't understand what you are doing, could you develop something different?" "This is Plan B because Plan A didn't work out. We need you to move to another city." Sound familiar? This passage from Genesis gives us the wonderful message that with God, *nothing* is ever arbitrary. Abraham gave Lot first pick of the land, and, as could be expected, Lot took the best for himself. Abraham got Plan B. God, however, reaffirmed that he had a plan for Abraham's life. His life had a goal, a purpose, a meaning. That meaning was sheer gift. He didn't have to seize it like Lot, who calculated how to get the best for himself. My life—and yours—is also sheer gift. Despite the seeming arbitrariness, reversals, and frustrations, we are on a journey, and the journey has a goal. It doesn't wind aimlessly around only to hit a dead-end. The destination is clear. Nothing will prevent us from reaching it as long as we, like Abraham, listen to God, obey his word, and worship him.

I am listening, trying to listen to you, the One who gives true meaning to my life. When I seem to be running in circles or to have hit a dead-end, let me hear your voice.

My Father's Hands

"I revealed your name to those whom you gave me out of the world. They belonged to you, and you gave them to me, and they have kept your word. Now they know that everything you gave me is from you, because the words you gave to me I have given to them, and they accepted them and truly understood that I came from you, and they have believed that you sent me. I pray for them. I do not pray for the world but for the ones you have given me, because they are yours, and everything of mine is yours and everything of yours is mine, and I have been glorified in them."

Jn 17:6–10 (NABRE)

————◆·◆·◆————

When people speak with me about death— their own impending death, whether they perceive it to be proximate or remote—their voice conveys trepidation, uncertainty, and fear. In this Gospel passage, from Jesus' last discourse, Jesus faces his own death with serenity. Serenity is the result of knowing that you cannot control the world around you or the time and manner of your death, but that you can nonetheless respond to and embrace what life—and death—brings you. Jesus' life and his death were by this time already in the hands of others, because Jesus allowed that in order to carry out the will of his Father. Above all Jesus knew he was also, always and forever, in the hands of his Father. Jesus makes it clear that we are also, always and forever, in the hands of the Father. We belong to the Father, consecrated and chosen from the beginning of the world. We belong to the Son, whose passionate love led him to throw himself into our midst and lift us to everything God had dreamt for us to have and to be. Although it is natural to tremble before the uncertainty of death, we can find hope in the reliability of Love who holds us and saves us forever.

Our Father, who art in heaven, hallowed—yes, forever hallowed—be thy name.

A Difficult Choice Made in the Dark

The people spoke against God and against Moses, "Why have you brought us up out of Egypt to die in the wilderness? For there is no food and no water, and we detest this miserable food." Then the LORD sent poisonous serpents among the people, and they bit the people, so that many Israelites died. The people came to Moses and said, "We have sinned by speaking against the LORD and against you; pray to the LORD to take away the serpents from us." So Moses prayed for the people. And the LORD said to Moses, "Make a poisonous serpent, and set it on a pole; and everyone who is bitten shall look at it and live."

NUM 21:5–8

———— ◆ · ◆ · ◆ ————

What would have happened if instead of complaining, the people had sought to see how God was acting *for* them in their frustrating desert experience? Throughout Numbers, the people complain and God often replies to their complaints, but never sympathizes with them. Instead, God said of those who muttered against him, "[They] have seen my glory and the signs that I did in Egypt and in the wilderness, and yet have tested me these ten times" (Num 14:22). These words show us that the opposite of muttering is not resignation (grin and bear it), but covenant relationship. God has also shown *us* his glory, working marvels for us. Instead of muttering complaints, which can come seemingly unbidden to our minds, we need to turn to our hearts. The heart asks questions. The heart seeks to understand and struggles to remain in relationship. When we encounter the vicissitudes that beset us on our desert pilgrimage to the Father, the devil wants nothing more than the grumblings that lead to distrust and rejection. Faith in God being with us and for us—a difficult choice always made in the dark—leads us to trust, acceptance, and peace.

Lord, instead of being disgusted with a situation, I will ask simply, Lord, what is going on here? Where are you? Show me your face, and I shall be saved.

Discovering Love

"[I]n all these things we are more than conquerors through him who loved us. For I am convinced that neither death, nor life, nor angels, nor rulers, nor things present, nor things to come, nor powers, nor height, nor depth, nor anything else in all creation, will be able to separate us from the love of God in Christ Jesus our Lord."

Rom 8:37–39

———•·•·•———

Sometimes it seems that we need to move mountains to get ourselves to believe in God's love for us. I remember as a novice telling a venerable old superior that I thought I didn't believe God loved me. "My dear," she responded, "this is a truth of faith! You must believe it." After that I certainly didn't bring up the topic again! But in my heart, I wanted so much the reassurance of knowing God's love for me. I wished for a surefire method I could follow to feel God's love. *Fortunately* there isn't one. For if we could manipulate our feelings of God's presence so easily, it certainly wouldn't be God's love that we were experiencing. Whether we feel God's love or not, the fact is we *are* loved by God. Without that love we wouldn't exist, for we are completely dependent on God. While there is no method, there is a *secret* to discovering God's love. Divine love begins with desire and grows with faith.

Lord, show me your face. Pour into my soul all the love that you are. Whether I feel your love or not, I shall believe your love surrounds and holds me in existence. Nothing will shake this certainty.

A Truly Creative Act

In the sixth month the angel Gabriel was sent by God to a town in Galilee called Nazareth, to a virgin engaged to a man whose name was Joseph, of the house of David. The virgin's name was Mary. And he came to her and said, "Greetings, favored one! The Lord is with you." But she was much perplexed by his words and pondered what sort of greeting this might be. The angel said to her, "Do not be afraid, Mary, for you have found favor with God. And now, you will conceive in your womb and bear a son, and you will name him Jesus...." Then Mary said, "Here am I, the servant of the Lord; let it be with me according to your word."

LK 1:26–31, 38

Obedience is a creative activity. Mary's words to the angel, "Let it be with me according to your word," directly reflect the words of God the Creator, "Let it be" (see Gen 1:3). Certainly the

Creator acted in power as he called into being galaxies and sky, stars and grass, mountains and chipmunks, tigers and elephants, and finally, man and woman. It is easy to mistakenly think that to be creative, we need unhindered freedom. We want to call projects into being, to do as we please, to create something that will last and bear our name into the future, to develop ourselves and command others. Mary, however, shows us the authentic human way of participating in God's creative activity: "Let it be done to me." Obedience, surrender, receptivity, and the desire to play our part in salvation history, the part written just for us—these are truly creative acts, because we allow God to create in us and through us for others. We hand over to God, as Mary did, our bodies, minds, and wills, our hopes and dreams, our futures, sufferings, and successes.

Lord, by participating in your creative act, I am pulled out of the small future I've dreamt for myself and emerge onto the stage of salvation history which reaches far into the future and has no end. Let it be done to me.

The Path of Holiness

Although you have not seen him, you love him;
and even though you do not see him now, you
believe in him and rejoice with an indescribable
and glorious joy, for you are receiving the out-
come of your faith, the salvation of your souls....
Therefore prepare your minds for action; disci-
pline yourselves; set all your hope on the grace
that Jesus Christ will bring you when he is
revealed. Like obedient children, do not be con-
formed to the desires that you formerly had in
ignorance. Instead, as he who called you is holy,
be holy yourselves in all your conduct; for it is
written, "You shall be holy, for I am holy."

1 Pet 1:8–9, 13–16

⋯ ✦ ⋅ ✦ ⋯

Years ago I read about a business executive from
the United States who spent her vacation
working in a home she had founded for orphans in
another country. For her, vacation was a chance to
revitalize her life by doing what she really wanted

to do: help others. This was her path of holiness. I know a mother whose two children are challenged in different ways. One has Down syndrome and the other is waiting for a lung transplant. This is her path of holiness. I have another friend whose wife left him. He makes every decision for the good of their three little girls. In a simple way his loneliness is transformed into solitude with a rare contemplative depth. This is his path of holiness. We each walk our own paths of holiness, because *although we have not seen Jesus, we love him. Even though we do not see him now, we believe in him and follow him, hoping in a future of indescribable and glorious joy.*

Pluck me, Lord, out of ease and comfort. Take me into the depths where you give yourself to those who love you. Let me weather the storm in peace. Give me a ready ear, an open heart, a humble mind, and a firm will. I surrender all to you. Amen.

The First Offer of Love Still Stands

This day the LORD, your God, is commanding you to observe these statutes and ordinances. Be careful, then, to observe them with your whole heart and with your whole being. Today you have accepted the LORD's agreement: he will be your God, and you will walk in his ways, observe his statutes, commandments, and ordinances, and obey his voice. And today the LORD has accepted your agreement: you will be a people specially his own, as he promised you, you will keep all his commandments, and he will set you high in praise and renown and glory above all nations he has made, and you will be a people holy to the LORD, your God, as he promised.

DEUT 26:16–19 (NABRE)

◆ ◆ ◆ ◆

The word "command" sounds harsh to our post-modern ears. We think that commands inhibit our freedom. We erroneously define freedom as having no restrictions, with nothing to prevent us from living a self-invested, self-centered life. But the author of Deuteronomy states, instead, that freedom comes with a *covenant relationship* with God. We are free because we are delivered from what offends God. We are free because we are who we were created to be "in the beginning" (Gen 1:1). Those three clue words point to the trust and openness that existed between the first man and woman and God. God's love is irreversible. First expressed "in the beginning," divine love continues to offer itself over and over again through the history and prophets of Israel, through the life, death, and resurrection of Jesus, through each of our lives. God's first offer of love still stands: *I will be your God. Will you be my people?* (see Ezek 37:27)

Deliver me, my God, from all that offends you—in my thoughts, my way of expressing myself, behavior, affection—that I may be all you desire me to be.

Jesus Chooses You and Me

He went up the mountain and called to him those whom he wanted, and they came to him. And he appointed twelve, whom he also named apostles, to be with him, and to be sent out to proclaim the message, and to have authority to cast out demons. So he appointed the twelve: Simon (to whom he gave the name Peter); James son of Zebedee and John the brother of James (to whom he gave the name Boanerges, that is, Sons of Thunder); and Andrew, and Philip, and Bartholomew, and Matthew, and Thomas, and James son of Alphaeus, and Thaddaeus, and Simon the Cananaean, and Judas Iscariot, who betrayed him.

Mk 3:13–19

— • · · • —

Imagine a father looking for a lost child. Dad wants help, so he puts together a search party. However, instead of calling on the FBI, police, and detectives, the father chooses a gang member, a child, a homeless person who knows all the streets in town, a mother from the neighborhood, a thief, and a murderer just released from prison. This would certainly make the evening news! In fact, people would probably scoff: "He's crazy! He's ruining his chance of saving his child!" Others would claim these people couldn't be trusted to love his child the way the father does. Admittedly, a couple of these characters might turn out to be the heartbroken father's worst nightmare. This, however, is precisely what happened when Jesus appointed twelve uneducated, unprepared, and unlikely men to help him in the very delicate work of saving the human race. They themselves were part of the humanity that needed salvation. If Jesus wanted the job done right, why didn't he choose angels he could trust? What mystery that he entrusted himself instead to family, friends, disciples, and women "who provided for" him (Lk 8:3). Today he entrusts himself to you and me.

Never, Lord, will I complain about others in the Church. Now I see how you have trusted us from the beginning to carry out your Father's plan for salvation. Nothing we can do can destroy the power of that plan. Thy Kingdom come!

Broken Open with Glory

In the beginning when God created the heavens and the earth, the earth was a formless void and darkness covered the face of the deep, while a wind from God swept over the face of the waters.

Then God said, "Let there be light"; and there was light. . . .

Then God said, "Let us make humankind in our image, according to our likeness; and let them have dominion over the fish of the sea, and over the birds of the air, and over the cattle, and over all the wild animals of the earth, and over every creeping thing that creeps upon the earth."

So God created humankind in his image, in the image of God he created them; male and female he created them.

GEN 1:1–3, 26–27

＊ ・ ＊ ・ ＊

When God created us he took a risk, a big risk. He created us free. He gave us quite a bit of latitude. He let us experience a wonderful relationship with him, as he walked with Adam and Eve in the cool breeze of the garden. God wooed us with his presence that we might choose his love, and in that choice, choose what was best for ourselves. Anyone who has trusted another—friend, spouse, or child—only to have that trust betrayed, knows a tiny bit of what God was all about. From the beginning, then, God's position toward his creatures was one of infinite vulnerability and freedom. It had to be this way because this is characteristic of the way the Persons of the Trinity relate to one another. If they wanted us one day to live within that eternal dance of Trinitarian love, we needed to learn from the very beginning how to truly live and love. Jesus had to come to show us how to live in vulnerability and love. From his birth to his death he refused the way of power. Just as he, in the end, was resurrected and given glory at the Father's right hand, we too, in walking the way of love, will find our lives broken open with glory when we least expect it.

Break open my life, O Holy Trinity, in glory this day.

God's Treasured Possession!

For you are a people holy to the LORD your God; the LORD your God has chosen you out of all the peoples on earth to be his people, his treasured possession.

It was not because you were more numerous than any other people that the LORD set his heart on you and chose you—for you were the fewest of all peoples. It was because the LORD loved you and kept the oath that he swore to your ancestors. . . . Know therefore that the LORD your God is God, the faithful God who maintains covenant loyalty with those who love him and keep his commandments, to a thousand generations. . . .

DEUT 7:6–9

----- • - • • - • -----

My brother is a police officer. One day he alerted me to an online video of college students being interviewed during a campus riot in the town where he serves. Most of those interviewed said things like: "How dare the police stop our fun! What have the police ever done for you or me anyway?" We can be horrified at their attitude, but if we look closely, many adults have the same attitude on a larger scale: *Why do we have to follow the Ten Commandments? Why can't we do what we want and live the way we want?* Good question. Why do we have to obey God anyway? We are God's treasured possession, his people, holy to him, chosen, loved. God has been faithful to us throughout human history and will show this fidelity for all eternity. We obey God because we are his people. Submission expresses our recognition of our place in this special relationship, as well as our trust that God always intends our well-being. I can understand how some college students may not yet be at the point of taking the long view of life. But you and I? We live in the mystery of salvation history.

What wonder to be a child of God, a brother or sister of Jesus the Christ, a temple of the Holy Spirit!

Intimacy

When it was evening, he took his place with the twelve; and while they were eating, he said, "Truly I tell you, one of you will betray me." And they became greatly distressed and began to say to him one after another, "Surely not I, Lord?" He answered, "The one who has dipped his hand into the bowl with me will betray me. The Son of Man goes as it is written of him, but woe to that one by whom the Son of Man is betrayed! It would have been better for that one not to have been born." Judas, who betrayed him, said, "Surely not I, Rabbi?" He replied, "You have said so."

MT 26:20–25

How close Judas was to Jesus—within an arm's reach. Surely, if he asked Jesus the question, *It is not I, Lord, is it?* he would have had to look directly into the Savior's eyes. Usually such intimacy produces trust and love. Although Judas held a particular place in the history of salvation, in a certain sense he represents all of sinful humanity. Who of us has not at some time rejected complete and trustful obedience to God? Who of us has not looked out for our own best interests, afraid to look directly into our God's eyes? We too are close enough to Jesus to share his table. We eat his Body and drink his Blood. But when we look in those eyes we know something Judas did not know at that Pasch. Even if we betray our Lord and Savior, even if we sell him for "thirty pieces of silver" (Mt 26:15), those eyes of love will never stop looking into our hearts. Humanity learned that mysterious and mind-blowing reality only after the death and resurrection of Jesus. The betrayal of our sin brings about the absolute proof of infinite compassion. God is mightier than our puny efforts at independence and our foolish attempts at power. So let us dip our hand into the dish with Jesus, that the closeness and the intimacy might melt away our selfish desires once and for all.

My Lord, remind me that I am ever within an arm's reach of infinite compassion and forgiveness.

The Free Follower of Providence

[S]omeone said to him, "I will follow you wherever you go." And Jesus said to him, "Foxes have holes, and birds of the air have nests; but the Son of Man has nowhere to lay his head." To another he said, "Follow me." But he said, "Lord, first let me go and bury my father." But Jesus said to him, "Let the dead bury their own dead; but as for you, go and proclaim the kingdom of God." Another said, "I will follow you, Lord; but let me first say farewell to those at my home." Jesus said to him, "No one who puts a hand to the plow and looks back is fit for the kingdom of God."

Lᴋ 9:57–62

———•·•·•———

Like these would-be followers of Jesus, we also, too often, have it all wrong. Children of rationalism, we think that it is *we* who decide to follow, *we* who understand, *we* who choose. We submit the mystery to our intellectual mastery. Jesus instead replied that mastery has no place in the mystery of salvation. "The Son of Man has nowhere to lay his head." Jesus had no control even over where he would sleep each night. He was the free follower of the Providence that takes care of sparrows and dresses the fields with flowers. Jesus was complete receptivity. Jesus was total obedience. In a world that judges everything by its own criteria of importance and worth, Jesus had no property, security, or credentials. He remained the everlasting child of the Father and said that those who follow him must also become children—small, trusting, having no need to build themselves up or show themselves off. Saint Thérèse understood this childhood, writing in her *Story of a Soul*, "[Lord,] for me to love you as you love me, I would have to borrow your own love. . . . I cannot conceive a greater immensity of love than the one which it has pleased you to give me freely, *without any merit on my part*."

Lord, make of me, work through me, give to me, only and always what you desire.

Declaring Our Commitment

Now when Jesus came into the district of Caesarea Philippi, he asked his disciples, "Who do people say that the Son of Man is?" And they said, "Some say John the Baptist, but others Elijah, and still others Jeremiah or one of the prophets." He said to them, "But who do you say that I am?" Simon Peter answered, "You are the Messiah, the Son of the living God."

Mt 16:13–16

This was a major turning point in the Gospel. The Twelve had been following the Teacher. They had witnessed miracles, heard him teach, watched him pray. But now, they had to step out of the shadows and bring into sharp focus who Jesus was for them. "Who do you say that I am?" Their answers determined their level of commitment. After Peter's answer he could no longer go back to the happy early days of Jesus' ministry with the crowds following him in astonished praise. No.

Now Jesus spoke of his passion, of the commitment demanded of anyone who wishes to share in his life. For us also, God is often in the background of our lives. Situations arise when we have to declare our level of commitment to the Lord. From that point forward he becomes central to our lives, not immediately, but in a gradual daily re-choosing of his way.

Master, you are everything for me. I want to be entirely for you. May I look into your eyes and promise you my love until my last breath.

God Will Do It Himself

Now may our God and Father himself and our Lord Jesus direct our way to you. And may the Lord make you increase and abound in love for one another and for all, just as we abound in love for you. And may he so strengthen your hearts in holiness that you may be blameless before our God and Father at the coming of our Lord Jesus with all his saints.

1 Thess 3:11–13

—— ◆ · · · ◆ ——

Contrary to what you've been told, *you* can't do it. You can't live a moral life. You can't obey God's law. As Saint Augustine said, it is not in our power to live as God desires. So give up trying and *start praying*. Paul prayed for his beloved Christians in Thessalonica: "And may *the Lord* make you increase and abound in love ... may *he* so strengthen your hearts in holiness that you may be blameless before our God and Father" (emphasis added). Perhaps that is why Paul was so full of gratitude. He knew that God wanted to give him what he couldn't do himself. Paul needed to pray, ponder, love, hope, and live in love with Jesus who had sought him out. If he continuously turned himself over to God's power, God would transform him in that power into all God desired. I once found a prayer that would make us fly on the path of holiness: "Lord, accomplish in me, yourself, all that you desire of me."

Lord, I can't do it. Most of the time I forget this, but whether I remember it or not, you want to do in me what I can't do. Lord, accomplish in me, yourself, all that you desire of me.

Becoming a Neighbor

But wanting to justify himself, he asked Jesus, "And who is my neighbor?" Jesus replied, "A man was going down from Jerusalem to Jericho, and fell into the hands of robbers. . . . Now by chance a priest was going down that road; and when he saw him, he passed by on the other side. So likewise a Levite, when he came to the place and saw him, passed by on the other side. But a Samaritan while traveling came near him; and when he saw him, he was moved with pity. . . . Which of these three, do you think, was a neighbor to the man who fell into the hands of the robbers?" He said, "The one who showed him mercy."

Lk 10:29–33, 36–37

If you are like me, I begin the day with too many things to do, back-to-back meetings, and a list of people I want to avoid because I know they'll upset my schedule. Like the man who asked Jesus, *So, who is my neighbor,* I too want to narrowly define neighbor, squeezing it into the few people and interruptions I can reasonably deal with. Jesus, however, is not interested in that question. In fact, he doesn't even answer it. After his tale of the man beaten and left for dead on the side of the road, Jesus asks a different question: *In this story, who has been the neighbor?* It is not a question of selecting those to whom I will dole out a few moments of compassion during the day. It is a matter of realizing that I need to become the neighbor who, despite inconvenience, expense, and unmet deadlines, drops everything to attend to another's need. Indeed, my final judgment will be based precisely on this: feeding the hungry, visiting the imprisoned, clothing the naked.

Lord, I beg you, let me be a neighbor to someone today.

It Isn't Crazy

Then he went home; and the crowd came together again, so that they could not even eat. When his family heard it, they went out to restrain him, for people were saying, "He has gone out of his mind."

Mk 3:19–21

------•-•••-•------

This is a perplexing Gospel passage. Why did Jesus' relatives think he was crazy? Here he was—an amazing healer, teacher, and prophet surrounded by disciples and sought after by crowds. Was it because he was so busy that he seemed to reserve no time for himself? Or was he attracting too much attention and putting himself or them at risk? Or was it perhaps the same thing that makes *us* wonder if Jesus is crazy? Love your enemies (see Mt 5:44).... Let anyone among you who is without sin be the first to throw a stone (see Jn 8:7).... Moses allowed you to write a bill of divorce, but it was not that way from the beginning (see Mk

10:4–5). . . . Take up your cross (see Lk 9:23). . . . You cannot serve God and wealth (see Mt 6:24). . . . The first will be last (see Mt 20:16). . . . Doesn't Jesus understand how utterly impossible these things sound? Has *he* felt human passions and been hurt at a brother's hands? We forget he has. Jesus knows that what he asks *sounds* crazy, because we can't do it alone. Only if we are grafted onto Jesus the living Vine will we be able to bear the living fruit he is talking about.

I'm a little shamefaced, Jesus. I have not always lived according to these seemingly crazy commands of yours. Give me today some time apart to shape my priorities and values according to your heart.

Drawn to New Depths

"And now, Lord . . . grant to your servants to speak your word with all boldness, while you stretch out your hand to heal, and signs and wonders are performed through the name of your holy servant Jesus." When they had prayed, the place in which they were gathered together was shaken; and they were all filled with the Holy Spirit and spoke the word of God with boldness.

ACTS 4:29–31

----•••••----

The Acts of the Apostles records God's great show of power through the prayer and ministry of the Apostles. This should wake us up to the power of God that breaks upon us when we worship as a community and minister in God's name. We Christians are too unaware of the power of the name we invoke. If we truly understood the liturgy we celebrate, our church buildings would rock. We would stop walking into church with such low expectations, that nothing much could happen. In reality, God might just draw us into new depths. God might take us to a place from which we could never return. But we're not waiting for the *buildings* where we worship to shake with the power of God. Instead, that power is about shaking our hearts. It can overturn our worlds of meaning, and make new sources of life and vitality spring forth. The overwhelming power of the Spirit of Jesus can do this! May my heart shake with the power of God that breaks upon me!

Break open, Lord, our slumbering, stony hearts and shape for yourself a new people!

The World Cries Out

The one who comes from above is above all; the one who is of the earth belongs to the earth and speaks about earthly things. The one who comes from heaven is above all. He testifies to what he has seen and heard, yet no one accepts his testimony. Whoever has accepted his testimony has certified this, that God is true. He whom God has sent speaks the words of God, for he gives the Spirit without measure. The Father loves the Son and has placed all things in his hands. Whoever believes in the Son has eternal life; whoever disobeys the Son will not see life, but must endure God's wrath.

Jn 3:31–36

I n this passage we eavesdrop on Nicodemus and Jesus talking about the witness of belief in the midst of the world. People enter into this dialogue between faith and culture in three different ways. Some suffer from a failure of nerve and build a fence around the faith, protecting it lest the culture contaminate it. Others make the faith over in the image of the culture, baptizing cultural expressions in the name of the Gospel. The third group, however, has enough trust in faith to get involved in the culture without identifying with it. They offer a particular kind of resistance and challenge to the culture. "And we are witnesses to these things, and so is the Holy Spirit whom God has given to those who obey him" (Acts 5:32). "Whoever believes in the Son has eternal life." The world needs witnesses. It cries out despite itself for people of courage, willing to confront it with "the one who comes from heaven." For somehow the world knows that in the end, only life open to the eternal can be called life at all.

May I open my heart wide to the world, inviting all to come to the feast the Savior sets. May all find in me consolation, compassionate guidance, and healing love.

A Tremendous Adventure

"Those who try to make their life secure will lose
it, but those who lose their life will keep it. I tell
you, on that night there will be two in one bed;
one will be taken and the other left. There will be
two women grinding meal together; one will be
taken and the other left."

Lk 17:33–35

———•·•·•———

This Gospel passage could be a rather grim
read—destruction, sin, fire and brimstone, losing life, a sudden visitation of the Son of Man that
separates one from another. . . . Every passage of
Scripture, however, needs to be seen in light of the
whole. The readings at a recent funeral of one of
our sisters could be read as a foil to this Gospel passage: "The voice of my beloved! Look, he comes. . . .
My beloved speaks and says to me: 'Arise, my love,
my fair one, and come away . . .'" (Song 2:8ff.). And
". . . a woman came with an alabaster jar of very
costly ointment of nard, and she broke open the jar

and poured the ointment on his head" (Mk 14:3ff.). Read side by side with our Gospel passage, these readings point out that Christianity, although lived out within the Christian community, is an almost terrifying personal responsibility as well as a tremendous adventure of life and love. By ourselves we cannot live a God-like life. We lose our life, which Jesus calls his followers to do, so that we can be brought back to life by God. And that new life is as fragrant as an expensive perfume and as promising as newly-wedded love.

Take my life, Lord, and use it. Draw me and I will run after you.

Bring Them to Jesus

When they came to the crowd, a man came to him, knelt before him, and said, "Lord, have mercy on my son, for he is an epileptic and he suffers terribly; he often falls into the fire and often into the water. And I brought him to your disciples, but they could not cure him." Jesus answered, "You faithless and perverse generation, how much longer must I be with you? How much longer must I put up with you? Bring him here to me." And Jesus rebuked the demon, and it came out of him, and the boy was cured instantly.

Mt 17:14–18

- - • - • • - • - -

Sometimes I find myself acting like these disciples. Just as this father brings his epileptic son to the disciples of Jesus to be healed, friends might bring me their struggles or a stranger might ask for prayers. When this happens, I feel responsible for conjuring up the miracle that will save the situation or heal the broken heart. I can imagine the disciples in Jesus' absence trying to figure out what to do, maybe trying a few things they had seen their Master do. But when Jesus arrives on the scene the father runs and throws himself at his feet with the utmost dependence and confidence. He had brought his boy to the disciples only because he believed they would bring him to Jesus, not try to figure out some makeshift human solution of their own. How embarrassed I feel before Jesus, when I realize I have tried to create miracles on my own. People really want to be brought to Jesus.

Lord, help me become, in some mysterious way, a pipeline for you to exercise your divine activity today.

What Is the Kingdom of God Like?

He said therefore, "What is the kingdom of God like? And to what should I compare it? It is like a mustard seed that someone took and sowed in the garden; it grew and became a tree, and the birds of the air made nests in its branches." And again he said, "To what should I compare the kingdom of God? It is like yeast that a woman took and mixed in with three measures of flour until all of it was leavened."

Lk 13:18–21

--- • • • ---

The two parables of the kingdom of God—the parables of the tiny mustard seed and the yeast—are not simply nice images meant to evoke imagination. Parables are explosive accounts of what is most true. The kingdom of God will take root, as a tree, and transfigure this world. Like yeast, it will penetrate governments, education, philosophy, financial enterprises, families, and human hearts. The daily news convinces us this is not happening. But Jesus promises us it is. When? The coming of the kingdom does not happen on our timetable, but on God's. Until the kingdom of God has become the kingdom of this world, Christians offer the world a visual parable of the kingdom of God. Those who do not yet believe must be able to see in our personal, family, and professional lives an answer to the question, "What is the kingdom of God like?"

How much trust you have in me, Jesus. You are trusting that my life will visually demonstrate the values and gifts of your kingdom. I am nothing without you. Shape my mind, will, and heart to be a sign of your love.

Living on a Larger Stage

The LORD is my light and my salvation;
  whom shall I fear?
... Though an army encamp against me,
  my heart shall not fear;
though war rise up against me,
  yet I will be confident.
Hear, O LORD, when I cry aloud,
  be gracious to me and answer me!
"Come," my heart says, "seek his face!"
... Do not give me up to the will of my
  adversaries,
    for false witnesses have risen against me,
    and they are breathing out violence.
I believe that I shall see the goodness of the LORD....

Ps 27:1, 3, 7–8, 12–13

———— ◆ · ◆ · ◆ ————

T he psalmist wrote this prayer when he was in
  great danger. He describes his fear with imagery that heightens in intensity: first he speaks of
fear; then he speaks of an army encircling him;

finally he uses the imagery of all-out war. Verse twelve tells us the cause of his anguish: he has been falsely accused, which at that time could lead to death. In this harrowing situation that must have filled him with mortal anguish, the psalmist still proclaims his belief that he shall see the goodness of the Lord. This psalm makes me think of Susanna in the Book of Daniel; of John the Baptist, Jesus, Peter, and Paul; of contemporary figures such as Anne Frank, Etty Hillesum, and Nelson Mandela. These individuals realized that the drama of their life was played out on a larger stage than their suffering alone. They discovered that they could bear everything and grow stronger through it, and that to live full of fear, anguish, bitterness, and hatred is truly to be deprived of life. They experienced that the loss of all one treasures in life, even the loss of one's life itself, has a deeper meaning. We must listen to our hearts, seek the Lord's face, and wait for him to act.

My soul, give praise to the Lord. All the days I live may I bless his holy name.

It's All about Love

When they had finished breakfast, Jesus said to Simon Peter, "Simon son of John, do you love me more than these?" He said to him, "Yes, Lord; you know that I love you." Jesus said to him, "Feed my lambs." A second time he said to him, "Simon son of John, do you love me?" He said to him, "Yes, Lord; you know that I love you." Jesus said to him, "Tend my sheep." He said to him the third time, "Simon son of John, do you love me?" . . . And he said to him, "Lord, you know everything; you know that I love you." Jesus said to him, "Feed my sheep. . . ." After this he said to him, "Follow me."

Jn 21:15–17, 19

Peter. We hear his first recorded words in the Gospel, "Go away from me, Lord, for I am a sinful man!" (Lk 5:8–10), to which Jesus responds, *Follow me.* We watch the Apostle later try to convince his Master not to go to his passion and death.

To which Jesus retorts, *Get behind me. You are not thinking as God thinks.* We are a bit taken aback when Peter states that he would die for Jesus, but then that very night denies he ever knew his Lord. Finally, we hear these last precious words between Peter and Jesus preserved in this Gospel passage. This time, however, the Lord begins the conversation. *Peter, do you love me?* Thrice he asks the brave Apostle who pledged his very life for Jesus this simple question that cuts to the quick: "Do you love me?" So this is what it is all about. *Love.* No great drama, accomplishments, or heroism. It's all about answering this longing of Jesus to be loved. That's all. And if we do love him, then we will hear with new ears the invitation he offers again and again: *If you love me, follow me.*

Yes, Lord, I love you. But I know I also am, like Peter, "a sinful man." Will you accept this humble offer of my heart?

Sustained by Intimacy

Jesus, knowing that the Father had given all things into his hands, and that he had come from God and was going to God, got up from the table, took off his outer robe, and tied a towel around himself. Then he poured water into a basin and began to wash the disciples' feet and to wipe them with the towel that was tied around him.

Jn 13:3–5

With these words John begins his account of the Last Supper. This particular account of the final meal before Jesus' death has become very meaningful to me. First, Jesus had a full schedule of ministry and knew his life was in danger. In the midst of all this Jesus stopped and called his followers together for a meal. He sought to comfort them and to derive support from the intimacy of the Passover meal. It wasn't a perfunctory following of the instructions for the Passover meal. Instead it began with a disconcerting act of humble hospitality. Jesus knew this was the last time before he died that he would be able to wash the feet of the men who had come to mean so much to him. He knelt before them with loving attention and tenderness. He spoke to them individually, as we see in his conversations with Peter and later with Thomas. Jesus—the giver of hospitality—has become my mentor. How can I provide a kind and welcoming invitation to others to relax, to be refreshed, to let themselves be cared for, to pause for times of intimacy, deep reflection, and feeling?

Jesus, help me stop worrying about my schedule so that I can create places of intimacy and hospitality where others may rest and we may be renewed together.

The Wine of Sorrow

Then the LORD answered Job out of the
whirlwind:
> ". . . I will question you, and you shall
>   declare to me.
> "Where were you when I laid the foundation of
>   the earth?
>   Tell me, if you have understanding. . . ."

Then Job answered the LORD:
> "I know that you can do all things,
>   and that no purpose of yours can be
>   thwarted. . . .
> Therefore I have uttered what I did not
>   understand,
>   things too wonderful for me, which I did
>   not know. . . .

JOB 38:1, 3–4; 42:1–2, 3B

A fter we reach a certain age, none of us can look
into the mirror without remembering the
dark wine of sorrow in our lives. Disillusionment,
anger, frustration, and bitterness may have filled

our thoughts and hearts as we struggled through days, weeks, and years of pain. Looking back, was there any meaning to it all? Have you ever asked God, *why?* Has God answered you? Are you still angry? Do you feel cheated in life? Have you found a resolution to the pain? Has it changed you, molded your character, made you more understanding of others, more gentle, more kind? This passage from the Book of Job shows us some remarkable things about God. First, God holds us in such esteem that he speaks to us directly about our pain. Second, not one tiny thing escapes God's attention. Like the most observant mother, God knows every detail of what happens to each of us. Third, our complaints about what happens to us are like the prattling of a child. We forget that in some mysterious fashion, nothing can thwart the purposes of God. Lastly, it is often only in the struggle initiated through suffering that we come to the point of truly seeing God.

Lord, I long to hear your voice. Come into the temple of my heart that I may receive you, worship you, be taught by you.

Beginning Again

I will now allure her,
>   and bring her into the wilderness,
>   and speak tenderly to her. . . .
There she shall respond as in the days of her
    youth,
>   as at the time when she came out of the
>   land of Egypt.
On that day, says the LORD, you will call me,
"My husband," and no longer will you call me,
"My Baal." For I will remove the names of the
Baals from her mouth, and they shall be men-
tioned by name no more. . . . And I will take you
for my wife forever; I will take you for my wife in
righteousness and in justice, in steadfast love,
and in mercy. I will take you for my wife in faith-
fulness; and you shall know the LORD.

Hos 2:14–17, 19–20

— • • • • —

Since I discovered this passage over thirty years
ago, I have come back to the wonderful book of
Hosea again and again. This book describes God's

relationship with his Chosen People as a marriage in which the wife has committed adultery. The husband takes her back repeatedly, only to have her leave him in search of other lovers. Hosea is saying that Israel, the bride of God, is accused of adultery because she has followed idols and relied on foreign nations and their gods for protection. Punishment was sure to come, a punishment meant to save them. Under no circumstances could Israel be considered a "virgin"; she is rather an unfaithful wife. However, God calls out to Israel to woo her as a man tries to win over a woman to be his bride. God has forgotten her adulterous past—he promises to abolish it—and is ready to begin again. In his new marriage with Israel he will make her a new creature. The story of Israel is the story of God's relationship with each of us.

In an instant, O God, you can abolish my past, my wayward ways, choices that led me down paths far from you. In an instant you can bring me back to you. You can throw the past away, never to be brought up again. We can begin again, Lord. You and I. Amen.

The Great Parade

[A] great crowd gathered around [Jesus]; and
he was by the sea. Then one of the leaders of the
synagogue named Jairus came and, when he saw
him, fell at his feet and begged him repeatedly,
"My little daughter is at the point of death.
Come and lay your hands on her, so that she
may be made well, and live." So he went with
him. And a large crowd followed him and
pressed in on him. Now there was a woman
who had been suffering from hemorrhages for
twelve years.... She had heard about Jesus, and
came up behind him in the crowd and touched
his cloak, for she said, "If I but touch his clothes,
I will be made well."

MK 5:21–25, 27–28

———•·◆·•———

Can you imagine the parade? The joy in the air?
The curiosity? The expectation? Jesus had
been preaching and working miracles wherever he
went. When Jesus arrived in this area by boat, he

began to teach the crowd. A father came up and asked him to come to his home to heal his daughter. So he dropped everything and went with the distraught man. In the jostling crowd a woman tried to get a cure without anyone knowing: *I'll just touch his cloak, then I'll slip away and no one will see me.* What was Jesus like this day? What were his attitudes? Was he smiling? Was he talking to the people nearest him? Did he listen interestedly to them? Or was he wishing for his own personal time and space, that everyone would go away and leave him alone? Too often *I'm* the grumpy one, overwhelmed by the requests of those who want help, a talk, a book, assistance with a project. I sure can't picture Jesus going about his ministry that way. This was why he came! To give his life and his love to those who needed it. He would go anywhere or do anything for someone who requested his help, surrendered their life to him, believed, repented.

Jesus, help me give myself to others as you did.

Keep on Loving

Now as [Saul] was going along and approaching Damascus, suddenly a light from heaven flashed around him. He fell to the ground and heard a voice saying to him, "Saul, Saul, why do you persecute me?" He asked, "Who are you, Lord?" The reply came, "I am Jesus, whom you are persecuting. But get up and enter the city, and you will be told what you are to do." . . . Saul got up from the ground, and though his eyes were open, he could see nothing. . . . So Ananias went and . . . laid his hands on Saul and said, "Brother Saul, the Lord Jesus, who appeared to you on your way here, has sent me so that you may regain your sight and be filled with the Holy Spirit."

ACTS 9:3–6, 8, 17–18

- - • • • - -

Paul is loved without limit. Paul responds by loving without limit. It's not that he went blazing through the world accomplishing a great project he had developed to prove his love for God. God wouldn't allow him to make that mistake! On the road to Damascus where God revealed Jesus to Paul, he said: *I have this vocation for you, Paul. Go into the city and there you will be told about it.* God sent Paul to the community of Christians, the very people he had come to imprison, the followers of the Way whom he despised. Jesus incorporated him into this community not as a celebrated hero, but as the least, as one accepted though not worthy, as one forgiven and reconciled. Jesus made him wait. Jesus made him dependent. Jesus let him experience the love of the Christian community, as well as the friction, as Paul sought to evangelize the Gentiles. In the midst of his everyday experience, Paul kept loving. This is his message to us. Different events and situations punctuate our days and shape our lives. Our business is to keep loving. In chaos . . . love. In misunderstandings . . . love. In affection . . . love in Christ. In joy and in sorrow . . . love. Always love. Love in all things. Love more. Never stop loving.

Show me, Lord, how I can love more. When my heart wants to shrivel in sorrow, jealousy, or anger, open it to the horizons and rewards of love.

Someone Is Waiting
for Your Story

They went to Capernaum; and when the sabbath came, he entered the synagogue and taught. They were astounded at his teaching, for he taught them as one having authority, and not as the scribes. . . . They were all amazed, and they kept on asking one another, "What is this? A new teaching—with authority! He commands even the unclean spirits, and they obey him." At once his fame began to spread throughout the surrounding region of Galilee.

MK 1:21–22, 27–28

———— • • • • ————

Ah! The "grapevine" at its best. Without e-mail, phones, the post office, Internet, or social media, the word got out. *Have you heard the latest? There is a new teacher in town. No one told you? You should hear how he speaks. My heart was moved like never before. And as if that weren't enough, he even healed someone with an unclean spirit, right there in the synagogue! Maybe he can cure your mother!* With all the means of communication we have, the grapevine is still the most personal way to catch up on the latest. What runs through our grapevines? Gossip, scandal, the latest news items? What would happen if we, like these ancient Galilean settlers, filled our grapevines and rumor mills with what God has done for us? Two thousand years ago the rumor mill got crowds to come out and listen to Jesus. Curiosity, interest, and desire drew them. They discovered that these rumors were actually true. The stories on the grapevine caused people to hope, to trust, to long for peace, to desire to change. These little messages created a movement. Do you have an experience of God's love you could share? Someone might just be waiting for your story!

Lord, we need you now. How can I speak of you so that others will want to listen? What means do I have at my fingertips that will help me share your love? Are you calling me to this?

Also by Kathryn J. Hermes, FSP

Reclaim Regret: How God Heals Life's Disappointments

Encounter the healing love of Jesus through scriptural prayer, stories, meditations, and reflections, and experience for yourself that God can transform even our deepest regrets and bring us freedom.

0-8198-6513-3   192 pages $14.95 U.S.

Jesus: Mercy from God's Heart

Beautiful reflections on the merciful love of Jesus as shown in the Gospels, the devotion of the saints, and in the stories of people today. Includes prayers to the Sacred Heart, Divine Mercy, and other prayers of intercession for mercy.

0-8198-4015-7   144 pages $7.95 U.S.

Surviving Depression:
A Catholic Approach

A reassuring approach to living through depression, which has helped thousands of readers. Translated into twelve languages.

0-8198-7225-3   192 pages $14.95 U.S.

Also in the Just a Minute Series

Meditations for Inner Peace

by Sr. Kathryn J. Hermes, FSP

Fifty scriptural meditations to help you grow in the peace that comes from seeing the events of life in the light of God's love.

0-8198-4982-0   112 pages $5.95 U.S.

Meditations to Grow in Self-Esteem

by Sr Marie Paul Curley, FSP

Fifty scriptural meditations to improve self-esteem by coming to truly believe in God's great love for you.

0-8198-4986-3   112 pages $5.95 U.S.

BOOKS & MEDIA

A mission of the Daughters of St. Paul

As apostles of Jesus Christ,
evangelizing today's world:

We are CALLED to holiness
by God's living Word and Eucharist.

We COMMUNICATE the Gospel message
through our lives and through all
available forms of media.

We SERVE the Church
by responding to the hopes and needs
of all people with the Word of God,
in the spirit of St. Paul.

For more information visit www.pauline.org.

BOOKS & MEDIA

The Daughters of St. Paul operate book and media centers at the following addresses. Visit, call, or write the one nearest you today, or find us at www.paulinestore.org.

CALIFORNIA
3908 Sepulveda Blvd, Culver City, CA 90230   310-397-8676
3250 Middlefield Road, Menlo Park, CA 94025   650-562-7060

FLORIDA
145 S.W. 107th Avenue, Miami, FL 33174   305-559-6715

HAWAII
1143 Bishop Street, Honolulu, HI 96813   808-521-2731

ILLINOIS
172 North Michigan Avenue, Chicago, IL 60601   312-346-4228

LOUISIANA
4403 Veterans Memorial Blvd, Metairie, LA 70006   504-887-7631

MASSACHUSETTS
885 Providence Hwy, Dedham, MA 02026   781-326-5385

MISSOURI
9804 Watson Road, St. Louis, MO 63126   314-965-3512

NEW YORK
115 E. 29th Street, New York City, NY 10016   212-754-1110

SOUTH CAROLINA
243 King Street, Charleston, SC 29401   843-577-0175

TEXAS
No book center; for parish exhibits or outreach evangelization, contact: 210-569-0500, or SanAntonio@paulinemedia.com, or P.O. Box 761416, San Antonio, TX 78245

VIRGINIA
1025 King Street, Alexandria, VA 22314   703-549-3806

CANADA
3022 Dufferin Street, Toronto, ON M6B 3T5   416-781-9131